May 25, 20

For M16

In the spirit of healing.
All the best,
Richard Bean

How JFK Killed My Father

PEARL POETRY PRIZE SERIES

London Underground • Richard Robbins
Gerald Locklin, Judge, 1989

Being the Camel • Angela Kelly
Laurel Speer, Judge, 1990

Cafés of Childhood • R. Nikolas Macioci
Robert Peters, Judge, 1991

Steubenville • Julie Herrick White
Donna Hilbert, Judge, 1992

Reflections of a White Bear • Carolyn E. Campbell
R. Nikolas Macioci, Judge, 1993

The Wave He Caught • Rick Noguchi
Ann Menebroker, Judge, 1994

How the Sky Fell • Denise Duhamel
Suzanne Lummis, Judge, 1995

Before Our Very Eyes • Cherry Jean Vasconcellos
Michael C Ford, Judge, 1996

Spontaneous Breasts • Nin Andrews
Denise Duhamel, Judge, 1997

One on One • Tony Gloeggler
W.R. Wilkins, Judge, 1998

Fluid in Darkness, Frozen in Light • Robert Perchan
Ed Ochester, Judge, 1999

From Sweetness • Debra Marquart
Dorianne Laux, Judge, 2000

Trigger Finger • Micki Myers
Jim Daniels, Judge 2001

RICHARD M. BERLIN

HOW JFK KILLED MY FATHER

[signature]

WINNER OF THE
2002 PEARL POETRY PRIZE
selected by LISA GLATT

Pearl Editions

LONG BEACH, CALIFORNIA

Library of Congress Control Number: 2003104800

Copyright © 2004 by Richard M. Berlin
All Rights Reserved
Printed in the United States of America

ISBN 1-888219-24-6

The poems in this book are products of the author's imagination. Names and characters are fictional and any resemblance to actual persons, living or dead, is entirely coincidental.

Excerpt from "The Practice" by William Carlos Williams, from *The Autobiography of William Carlos Williams*, copyright © 1951 by William Carlos Williams. Reprinted by permission of New Directions Publishing Corporation.

"How JFK Killed My Father" originally appeared in *Psychosomatic Medicine* 62 (2000): 219, copyright © 2000 by Lippincott Williams & Wilkins. Reprinted by permission of the publisher.

"Our Medical Marriage" originally appeared in *Annals of Internal Medicine* 131 (1999): 711, copyright © 1999 by the American College of Physicians–American Society of Internal Medicine. Reprinted by permission of the publisher.

"Sleight of Hand" originally appeared in *JAMA: The Journal of the American Medical Association* 278 (1997): 1130af, copyright © 1997 by the American Medical Association. Reprinted by permission of the publisher.

Book design by Marilyn Johnson

Cover photo: Presidential motorcade, Mexico City, 1962
Cecil Stoughton, White House photographer
Courtesy of the John Fitzgerald Kennedy Library, Boston

PEARL EDITIONS
3030 E. Second Street
Long Beach, California 90803
U.S.A.

For My Father

Acknowledgments

Many of the poems in this volume first appeared in *Psychiatric Times* (www.psychiatrictimes.com) and its younger sibling, *Medicine & Behavior*. I am deeply thankful to John L. Schwartz, M.D., Editor-in-Chief, and Christine Potvin, Editorial Director, for creating the column "Poetry of the Times" to feature my work. Additional thanks to Henry Tulgan, M.D. for publishing my poems as a regular feature of the *Berkshire Medical Journal*.

I would also like to thank the editors of the publications in which the following poems previously appeared:

American Journal of Nursing: "Blighted Ovum"
Annals of Internal Medicine: "Our Medical Marriage"
Artful Mind: "Alzheimer's Unit," "Sleight of Hand"
Buckle &: "Sleight of Hand," "Alzheimer's Unit," "Code Blue," "What I Love"
Flyway: A Literary Review: "What a Dying Woman Saw"
JAMA: The Journal of the American Medical Association: "Sleight of Hand"
Journal of Family Practice: "Portrait of a Family Doctor"
Journal of General Internal Medicine: "What to Call Me"
Journal of Medical Humanities: "What a Dying Woman Saw"
The Lancet: "Berlin Wall"
Peregrine: "Tools"
Psychosomatic Medicine: "How JFK Killed My Father"
Ward Rounds: "Our Medical Marriage"
Western Journal of Medicine: "Code Blue"

A number of poems also appeared in *Code Blue*, winner of the Poetry Society of South Carolina Kinloch Rivers Memorial Chapbook Competition, 1999.

"Anatomy Lab" and "Sleight of Hand" appeared in *Holding True: an Anthology of Berkshire Poets* (Mad River Press, 1999).

"Our Medical Marriage" appeared in *This Side of Doctoring: Reflections from Women in Medicine* (Sage Publications, 2002).

Finally, thanks to my patients; and to Barry Sternlieb; Denise Duhamel; Marilyn Johnson; Cortney Davis; the Every Third Thursday Writer's Group—Cynthia Gardner, Michelle Gillett, Jan Hutchinson, Pat Ryan, Norah Walsh; Carol Mielo Swerzenski; Jan Bailey; Steve Bierman; Derek Stern; Michael Kronig; Basil Michaels; Ellen Eldridge; James Hill; Sandy McNay; Joshua Yurfest; Maria Sirios; Charles Harper Webb; Lisa Glatt; Daniel Berlin; Roslyn Berlin; Rachel King Berlin; and my wife, Susanne King.

Contents

Foreword by Lisa Glatt xi

I. LEARNING THE SHAPES

Anatomy Lab 3
Learning the Shapes 4
Uncle Joe 5
Sunday Parade 6
January Thaw 7
Inside Out 9
Open You Up 10

II. ROLE MODELS

My First Professor 13
Role Model 14
The Hotseat 15
The Way He Managed 16
What I Revealed 17
Before the Malpractice Suit 18
The George Washington Bridge 19
How JFK Killed My Father 20

III. CODE BLUE

PTSD 25
Unabomber 26
Code Blue 27
Places We Have Met 28
Radium Girls 29
Spring Planting 32
What a Dying Woman Saw 33
Two Portraits of AIDS 34
Apology 36
The Most Common Time 37
Piano Music 38
The Mask 39

IV. WHAT A PSYCHIATRIST REMEMBERS

Alzheimer's Unit 43
First Break 44
Tools 46
Woman with a Finger Stuck in Her Nose 47
Migration, 3 A.M. 48
Transference 49
Crossing the Street 50
What a Psychiatrist Remembers 52
Rough Air 54
What Makes a Psychiatrist Cry 55
Berlin Wall 56
Dance Lesson 57
Covert Operations 58
Jumpology 59

V. WHAT I LOVE

If You Ask Me My Name 63
Sleight of Hand 64
Obstetrics Ward, County Hospital 65
Hospital Food 66
The Tailors of Children's Memorial 67
Portrait of a Family Doctor 69
Sleep Lab Meditation 70
Blighted Ovum 71
Our Medical Marriage 73
After Watching *Chicago Hope* 74
What I Love 75

Foreword

IF YOU ASK RICHARD BERLIN his name he will say "healer, priest, turner of textbook pages, searcher, listener, arrogant crow costumed in white . . ." And if you ask me, I'll add poet.

How JFK Killed My Father introduces us to an important new voice in contemporary poetry and offers us a rare, poignant glimpse into one doctor's world through poems that are honest and unflinching, gentle and brutal at once. Berlin has viewed the human body and mind, not with a doctor's necessary detachment that I, for one, have felt when in my own paper gowns and booties, but with a sensitive and vivid tenderness. Berlin is a most insightful and generous witness, seeing and giving at the same time, and in reading him, one becomes a witness too. We're made aware of all that the body holds, clutches, gives up, and finally lets go of.

Here we have the beauty and the horror: *His face is a hideous bouquet of red tulips this morning.* Here we have frailties, not only of obviously ill patients, but of seemingly healthy doctors: *On the day he could not know/ would be his last, he traced healing scars/ with eye and fingertip, cut new wounds/ with clean hands, alive/ with the snap of latex gloves.* Here we have the end and the beginning: *how we die without appetite/ and the way we live with our hungers.*

Here we have a doctor who admits that to "save a life" is to pretend, a doctor who knows "it's just a postponement." Read Richard Berlin's poems; they are the salve. They are the music we hear while we wait.

—*Lisa Glatt*
Long Beach, California
June 2003

How JFK Killed My Father

. . . as a writer I have never felt that medicine interfered with me but rather it was my very food and drink, the very thing which made it possible for me to write. Was I not interested in man? There the thing was, right in front of me. I could touch it, smell it. It was myself, naked just as it was, without a lie, telling itself to me in its own terms. Oh, I knew it wasn't for the most part giving me anything very profound, but it was giving me the terms, basic terms with which I could spell out matters as profound as I cared to think of.

—William Carlos Williams

I.
Learning the Shapes

Anatomy Lab

She was stretched out naked,
young and blonde,
wild and frightening

when the others were so old,
everyone at the steel table
pretending not to notice

the fortune of her body.
That first day I sliced off her breast,
scalpel circling round and round

the way I might halve a peach,
to study her glistening secrets
with detachment and awe.

We explored the deep insertions
where muscle joins bone,
subtracted her face, her arms,

plucked ovaries and heart like thieves,
but lost count of the treasures
severed from ourselves.

By year's end, brittle as guilt,
we hovered over our hollow creation,
pretending to look away

from the short blonde braid
at the base of her skull
no one had the courage to cut.

Learning the Shapes

Five students
wear short white coats,
pockets bulging notecards,
tuning forks, new stethoscopes.
Demanding consent
we snap on latex gloves,
smear index fingers with K-Y,
turn them over, spread them apart
and enter alone, one by one
to learn the shapes inside:
smooth chestnut, soft orange,
stone in a muddy field.
After wiping off the jelly
we wash our hands clean,
examining fingers sensitive
as a blind bluesman
who hears each note
an instant before
touching a tight steel string.

Uncle Joe

What did I know of suffering's music,
a suburban boy with clean Converse All Stars
and pockets stuffed with new tools.
I was learning somewhere in the clouds,
the blue lake far below
the floor filled with jaundiced men.
The Chief gave me Uncle Joe,
"King of 18 West,"
95 and kept alive by each new breeze of students.
His hairless body lay smooth and contractured,
mouth torn in a silent scream,
face drawn tight on bones
like wet leather stretched and dried in the sun.
I hated to touch him, hated his smell,
the urine and helpless sweat,
sick when I suctioned
green horror from his body.
All I wanted was to let him die.

One morning, the clouds drifting,
I sang without conscience,
as if the man whose body I pierced for blood
had vanished to the sky.
And then I gasped at his breathing's new beat.
I sang louder, faster, my song, his rhythm
in gentle syncopation, voice off key,
mouth to his ear, warm breath on my cheek,
strong wings pounding.

Sunday Parade

Every day we tend them,
women and men wired to monitors,
people who have seen the white flash of light.
When they code at 2 A.M., alarms blasting,
we barricade death
with sweat, with lidocaine,
and the darkness of our humor.
And on Sunday mornings
we beautify with mortician flair:
sponge and powder,
lipstick glossed on cheeks,
a necklace, stickpins in their johnnies,
sit them up like kings and queens
on the red vinyl throne of a geri-chair.
To the music of the Gomco's suck
we hide tubes below blankets
and prop the *Times* on withered hands.
All for the Chief
with his clean white coat,
the strut and preen of his own parade.

January Thaw

It is the winter of chest pain and snow,
all the drunks smashed
through the ER doors.

The senior resident in his new blue coat
can coax a silent heart,
but only curses the jaundiced men,

exiles them to frozen doorways,
shivered Thunderbird,
the lukewarm comfort of bitter coffee.

And he hates Drunken Johnny most of all,
loathes him and saves him,
Johnny rising immortal in disregard

for the slum of his body.
One night, he stumbles in, explosive,
ice loaded on his beard,

snow like soot falling from his flak jacket.
He shuffles to the gurney,
the senior's rage like an ice storm.

Johnny's hands shake
to untie a glazed lace,
and when he grunts a drunken heave

on his boot, his foot breaks off
silent as torn moldy bread.
Johnny collapses, an intern vomits,

but the senior stands hard
until tears kick across his face
and he wails like spring rain for a surgeon.

Inside Out

Still fresh
with the smell of after-shave,
he sprawls in bed,
seersucker johnny worn backwards,
Plane & Pilot in his hand
wrapped in plastic.
He knows the date, the hospital,
can name Clinton, Bush, Reagan.
Ribbons lie on his night stand
where a gift box holds a paisley
sleeve pulled inside out.
He lifts the box,
studies the puzzle,
eyes ricocheting
from mine to the robe
as he lunges an arm
at the pulled-in sleeve.
Another lunge, another,
his arm sliding into air
as he shoves me away,
two men alone in a room,
helpless to reverse
a world pulled inside out.

Open You Up

The smile was fear.
Twenty pack-years and a few month's cough —
a steelworker from Gary,
X-ray lit with a lesion
round and opaque as a silver dollar.
I wanted to tell him,
to pull the curtain around us
and sit beside him on his bed,
to break the news
soft as a surgeon's hand.

But I swaggered and stood
like a half-drunk general:
You've got something in your chest
and we've got to open you up.
I can't remember his response,
just the flame in my cheeks
and our meeting months later,
his face the color of fly ash.
So much bone when he hugged me
like my father before he died,
the emptiness in my chest,
something opened up, forever.

II.

Role Models

My First Professor

I listened to my brother bark
like the start of a hunt.
After humidified weeks
breathing plumes of steam,
his cough suddenly stopped
and he turned a mottled blue.
I remember my mother's rush
to the phone, her call to Eli,
God himself, who arrived
with his scuffed black bag.
He ordered towels and hot water,
washed his satisfied hands
and entered our tropics with a stethoscope
circling his neck like a vine.
In the mist he moved the silver moon
across my brother's chest, listening
like a cellist with perfect pitch.
Back in clear air, he glanced at my mother
limp on the sofa and dialed the rotary phone:
Yes, an admission. One-year-old boy,
laryngotracheabronchitis.
In minutes, I heard the cat scream
of an ambulance, witnessed
a jungle of white-coated men.
Afterwards, alone at the neighbor's,
repeating that long word,
I unpacked my own black bag,
the tin foil mirror and pink sugar pills,
pressed the plastic stethoscope to my chest.

Role Model
   —for Eli Sheer, M.D.

Back then, doctors drove black Cadillacs
and kept office hours at home.
Week after week, seated on his leather table,
I watched Dr. Sheer boil three dull needles
in a silver tray, screw them to glass syringes,
suck yellow extracts of ragweed and dust
from clear bottles, and drive each point
home. How courageous I felt as I rolled up a sleeve,
smelled alcohol breathe from cotton balls,
kept my gaze steady on each pink welt.
And I loved the moment after,
when he scrubbed his hands,
reached into his desk drawer for a lollipop,
and printed the date and doses in long columns
with his gold-tipped fountain pen.

One afternoon, a fresh band-aid on my arm,
hands holding a football, the itch began
deep in my chest and throat, so deep
I wanted to swallow my hand and scratch.
I ran home to Mother who called him,
then dragged me, blue faced, to the office
where he sat with the sports section.
I smelled alcohol, felt the stings,
and when I turned pink, he exhaled slowly,
nodded to my mother, then picked up
the newspaper to finish his reading.

The Hotseat

I swear by Apollo the physician, and Aesculapius, and Hygeia and Panacea, and all the gods and goddesses . . . to reckon him who taught me this Art equally dear to me as my parents . . .
  —from the Hippocratic Oath

0700 and thirty housestaff collapse
like shipwreck survivors.
After 24 sleepless hours
of children renounced by Hygeia,
our eyes are drowned in shadow.
A few nod before he enters
ruddy-faced and rested,
white coat starched and spotless:
Dr. Harry, Chief of the Mecca,
diagnostic wizard, the power
who can crush careers with a word.
He slaps a chest film on the light box
and hooks a bleary intern:
Tell me, doctor,
what is the shape of this child's ears?
Fifteen seconds, thirty, a minute of silence,
sweat weeps from the intern's forehead.
Harry scorches him with questions
and solves the riddle like Aesculapius,
even kneads the intern's shoulders
as if soothing a bruise.
We curse him all day, stay awake
all night to earn his love,
and when we descend to Radiology
with our own tame students, we slap
a film on the light box and raise
their first beads of sweat.

The Way He Managed

With strong hands
and the burnished smell of leather
stacked to the ceiling on skids,
visored and aproned, knives honed
on hides they will trim into sweatbands,
the cutters begin their work.
They trace a rim of brass
guiding blade through calfskin
steady as a scalpel.
These men understand the grained voice
leather whispers to their hands,
the secret of where to cut,
the caress of skin on skin
in the heaven of a hat.
                    I was a boy who spent summers
stacking bands they cut, packed them into cases
by the gross, the boss's son they let watch from a distance.
My father chose hides from tanneries in Salem and Peabody
more carefully than some men choose wives,
knew bandsaws, bills of lading, and leather's brutal secrets.
And late afternoons, sun plunging through the skylight,
his strong hand relaxed on my shoulder,
we would watch the regular slice of men at work,
the tender smell of leather in the air.

What I Revealed

Because I like people and science and
want to relieve suffering in the inner city
was my song at med school interviews.
I might have left the applications blank

or fled to Canada
if my father hadn't flown a thousand miles
to persuade me to apply:
even then, I couldn't confide

how much I longed to save him.
Helpless since 12, I learned to recite
ulcerative colitis, hepatitis,
ileostomy, colostomy,

autoimmune hemolytic anemia
while cortisone shaped his face
to a full moon. When steroids raged,
he smacked my head with his wedding band,

but never saw me cry.
By the time I buttoned my white coat
his cancer grew everywhere,
and though I had learned the risk for others,

even held it hard and bloody in my hands,
I never thought to warn him —
still a son accustomed to revealing
less than everything.

Before The Malpractice Suit

We watch my father wake
for morning rounds —
so much blood lost
since he met this doctor
at a Boston Mecca.
Levered up on elbows,
arms shaking for strength,
my father tries to meet him
eye to eye, but the doctor stares
out the window, brags
of the miles he jogged
before breakfast, the beauty
my father missed
in the sky before dawn.
Without touch of word or hand,
the doctor rips a microcasette
from a holster on his hip
and chants the labs,
my father collapsing back,
each number a needle stick,
a scalpel's nick we remember
after all the blood is counted.

The George Washington Bridge

I stand beneath the bridge and listen
to it flex and sing
as traffic mourns overhead,
the water below
whipped into white scallops
by a fierce south wind.
Across the river, a city flows
on streets my father knew as a boy,
when men welded steel and fell
as they strained to connect
the yearning concrete spans.

On ribbon cutting day
he walked across,
the river clean and blue back then,
years before his commute
on the Red & Tan bus
over the bridge to his factory
filled with the smell of leather skins
he swore kept him alive
when rivers of blood
poured from his gut until he fell
silent, and I did not know
how to risk my life to reach him.

How JFK Killed My Father

Within recent medical times psychologic investigations have reawakened interest in the psychological settings in which illness develops. Reports in the literature have singled out loss as a precipitating factor in a variety of disorders . . . including ulcerative colitis.
—Arthur H. Schmale Jr., M.D.
in *Psychosomatic Medicine*

It was a time when men wore fedoras
banded on the crown, each band with a feather
tucked into a bow, and inside,
sweat bands carved from calfskins
with their sweet smell of animal and earth.
I remember the photo over my grandfather's desk,
a sepia-toned panorama shot
from his ninth-floor factory window,
Broadway below a surge of ticker tape
and hats tossed in the air for FDR,
hats pouring into the street, hats
waved in exaltation, hats
taking off like America.

After two war-time winters in Greenland
my father came home, hat in hand,
and bought the sweat band business,
made it grow like his young family,
presidents and hopefuls motorcading down Broadway:
Truman in a Scala wool Homburg,
Ike's bald head steamed in fur felt,
Stevenson's ideals lost in the glory
of a two-inch-brimmed Stetson.

But when thick-haired Kennedy
rode top down and bare-headed,
men all over America took off their hats
in salute, in praise and imitation,
flung them into the street forever.
Hat factories closed quiet as prayer books,
and loss lingered in my father's guts
like unswept garbage after a big parade.

Years later, yarmulke on my head,
they asked me to view him in his coffin.
I can still see his face shaved smooth as calfskin,
his dark suit, crisp white shirt and tie,
how I laughed that they dressed him for eternity
without a hat. And I can still hear
the old men murmur in the graveyard,
Kennedy did it to him,
fedoras held close to their leathered hearts.

III.

Code Blue

PTSD

For months she has dreamed in red:
blood flows from his mouth,
soaks his gown a deep red-brown.
She code blues a prayer,
stands aside as the team arrives
in ones and twos, breathless,
mouth blood pulsing.
Starched and spotless,
compressed in the doorjamb,
she is untouched
by the blood on their gloves,
the blood in the lines,
the blood spattered on white Nikes,
floor slick with cells and plasma.
Eyes locked on the flat-lined monitor,
she hears the last blood gurgle,
the team quiet and calm in a lake of blood.
And after they raise him on the cart,
she fills out the forms,
watches a woman mop,
hears soles stick to the floor,
the splash of pink water on steel.

Unabomber

He was headline news
the morning I told her,
eyes gone blank,
jaw dropped:
Just like my mother
she whispered at the door.

When she misses her follow-up
and misses it again
I conceal the words
breast cancer
in an envelope
I want to explode in her face.

Code Blue

I'm running
running the way we all run
toward death,
sprinting through swarms
of *Pseudomonas* and *Serratia*,
the din of the soaps,
a demented man's scream.

And I run the code
serene as a monarch,
issue edicts and commands,
infusions, boluses, electric thumps
until I drop the paddles,
bent, breathless.

When I raise my eyes,
the body on the bed,
dusky blue, spreads
limp as twilight
on the wintry hills outside,
commuter traffic on the street
choked motionless,
the silent signal light beating
amber, red, green.

Places We Have Met

I heard something like a whisper once
in grade school, a boy's blood
Thinned to water they said
as we stared at his empty seat.

When the first glass syringe
stuck to my father's arm
like an engorged tick
he smiled his lie: *Don't be afraid.*

Then bitter grandmother, diabetic blood
so sweet, lost a little toe,
a foot, her leg, until she groaned,
Let me go.

Or that first week in medical school,
the man my age, wheezing gray bones,
wife and kids holding wasted hands,
Something in his lungs.

And we touched, inevitable as lovers,
my finger in a latex glove
deep inside, rubbing over and over
something hard and common as a garden stone.

Now a friend loses her glorious hair,
my mother moans without a breast,
and my hands search hidden places
where something dark might live

but feel only cold through thin sheets,
a familiar whisper on my skin.

Radium Girls

1898

From a ton of pitchblende
dumped at the edge of pine woods,
Marie Curie fills her vats
and begins a four year stirring.
She boils hot miasma
down to thimbles of crystal radium
until the lab fills with the glow of decay.
At night, avoiding the moon's spell,
Marie and Pierre bathe
in flickering blue silhouettes
that glow in their tubes *like faint fairy lights.*
I can see them kiss like lovers before a fire,
passions aflame, her marrow burning to scar.

1917

Huddled in Belgian trenches
where time has stopped,
soldiers count the numbers
radiating from their watches,
deadly as mustard gas,
comforting as any light in darkness.
Back home, their sweethearts
long for safe returns, yearn
for glow-in-the-dark light pulls.

1918

Fifty girls hunch at wooden desks
in the Radium Dial Company, Ottawa, Illinois,
hair cut short, heads aligned like an army in review,
not a soldier older than 20,
wooden trays beside them filled with clocks
arranged like cupcakes waiting to be iced.
They mix paint from powdered base,
lip-point brushes with long licks
into tips fine enough to paint time,
two hundred fifty dials a day,
five and a half days each week,
a penny and a half per dial.
Covered with a thin powder
that *puts a glow in your cheeks*,
they paint their buttons, fingernails, teeth.
Beneath the stardust, boys gravitate
to their radiant blue bodies.

1925

Confused bones bond radium tight,
and it singes their core
until jaws break, teeth rot,
wounds grow purulent without healing.
The company claims safety.
Dentists lie through their teeth.
And one hundred Radium Girls are dead.

1938

A woman is stretched out on her sick bed.
Five former workers encircle her,
arms folded, looking down at the figure
whose eyes are closed and could pass for dead.
A dark-suited man sits and stares
directly at her closed eyes but doesn't touch her.
One woman holds a comma of white hand
while the others stand inert.
On the wall behind the group
hangs a cheap picture of a pine forest
my eyes search for a pile of pitchblende.

1998

Motherless since six, a 70-year-old daughter
walks her 5 A.M. mile to the Ottawa cemetery
and tends the grass on her mother's grave.
Argonne National Laboratory dug here last month.
Six feet down, bones still tick
in the earth's dark pocket.

Spring Planting
—for Julianna A. Luntz Van Raan, 1950–1998

A morning call wakes me
something hard and fibrous in her leg
growing fast and uncontrolled
that can't be weeded out.
Through my bedroom window
I study winter rye in April
swinging on strong stems.
I wish I could plant Julie's
leg in a warm tangle of earth,
turn her face toward the sun,
and let her nurse on spring rain
like the dandelions waiting
to fill the meadow with stars.

What a Dying Woman Saw

She was clear-eyed and dying
when I knew her, soft breaths feathering
from her chest like distant smoke,
face bleached white as burnt-out sky.
Propped in a chair, oxygen prongs pulled
to her neck, she commanded like a queen
for morphine, lobster, a second phone,
her mind still ruling an 80-pound body.
She allowed me to sit at the foot
of her bed like a commoner, let me ask
the details of lineage and disease,
revealed the smothering fear in her dream.
And on the last morning, when I'd suctioned
dark secretions, she wheezed,
You're a poet, aren't you?
That was before I thought to write
more than a patient's history in a chart,
before I knew what lets us breathe easier,
before their stories engraved me like stone.

Two Portraits of AIDS

1. FATHER PAUL

A crucifix hangs
safety-pinned to his sweater,
his hollow cheeks marked with scarlet lesions.
I've watched his body wither
to a shadow of his cane.
Parishioners pray for him,
but if he names his illness
they will stone him out of town.

Let's get this over with, he demands
when pneumonia moves into his bony chest.
The sister who speaks
only of the weather,
ignores his protests
and calls an ambulance.

He curses her,
laughs, *I'm ready.*
During pain-free moments
he has confessed,
written his obituary and funeral mass.
And he has cried
goodbye to his drunken father
who still believes
he has the flu.

Today he is here for our monthly visit,
waiting to start 3TC.
I watch him
strain like a weight lifter
to press his body
from the chair.
He stands,
catches the door frame,

brushes against the wall of diplomas,
clutches my desk top,
pauses for breath,
and finally, smiling,
makes a free fall plunge
into his usual seat.

2. WILLIAM

Six-two, maybe 220,
hints of scarlet on his handsome cheek,
and a voice that slams
through my office door,
cursing AZT
and doctors who don't return calls.
When the time comes, no heroics, okay?

Prozac, Ambien, Xanax
give no relief.
He scans the Internet
for new treatments:
3TC, Cytolin, Kombacha mushroom tea.
We agree about morphine
at the end.
He asks me what to do,
this man who will do anything:
Paint as often as before,
when your studio was a party,
your brushes loaded with paint.

He returns home
and stares out the farmhouse window,
spent as the weakened storm
in the north Atlantic,
kicking up waves,
drifting off
our local weather map.

Apology

High above a northern coast
I read my poems to Father Paul and William.
A cormorant speeds down a shore
lined with granite boulders
black as dead men's teeth.
I've been over my head in this winter sea,
bones aching cold from all the dead and dying
I've held this drowning year:
William's plastic tubes streaming like seaweed,
electricity burning Father Paul's legs,
his thin smile and spindled hand
trembling an offer of gold-wrapped chocolate.
My distant father drifts here, too,
always dying in Piscataway, New Jersey.
William paints now on a warmer coast
and believes he is cured.
Father Paul will die in his sleep,
and I'll cry survivor's guilt,
apologize for stealing their pain
for poems, ashamed of my living greed,
like a sailor flailing
for a piece of wreckage as he swallows
the ocean and his own tears,
a moaner buoy somewhere in the distance
the only voice he hears.

The Most Common Time

Death comes Monday morning, 9 A.M.
Nothing prepares you, a foot starts to shake
Wild as a storm cloud in a hard north wind.
Cold sweat on your forehead raises the stakes.

Nothing prepares you, a foot starts to shake
While sun on pale earth dismisses the frost.
Cold sweat on your forehead raises the stakes,
Your mind in the garden, denying all loss.

While sun on pale earth dismisses the frost,
Trees nail shadows to the walls of your home,
Yet your mind roams the garden, denying all loss.
Pain crushes your chest, you fall toward the phone,

Trees nail shadows to the walls of your home.
Wild as storm clouds in a hard north wind,
Pain crushes your chest. You fall by the phone.
Death comes Monday morning, 9 A.M.

Piano Music
—for Howard Kanner, M.D., 1945–1996

A flag at half-mast, tissues piled
in the OR lounge, the hallway gasps:
What were his risk factors?
No one dared say it out loud,
how we tallied our own frailties,
clear for an instant,
like skywriting before a wind.

On the day he could not know
would be his last, he traced healing scars
with eye and fingertip, cut new wounds
with clean hands, alive
with the snap of latex gloves,
the precise steel scalpel and rongeur.
Between cases, he confided in me:
a wish to learn piano, an instrument
where the choices are black and white.
And he laughed as he ate a peach,
the sugary juice glistening
on his hand, his tongue
tracing each scrubbed finger.
I don't know who he touched
between the pleasures of that taste
and the call to 911,
what music he heard as he waited.

The Mask

His face is a hideous bouquet
of red tulips this morning
before he moves to the other coast.
I unwrap his gift, a mask
fashioned from coarse brown paper,
eye holes shaped like tears,
with an elastic strap to bind
mask to skin like a bandage.
It's the mask of Mil Mascaras,
a wrestler who hid the secret
of his face until the last fight.
He leans toward me with the story:

Mascaras sits alone in his dressing room,
chair missing a rung, white porcelain sink
dripping blue stain, heat pipes a hundred degrees,
the crowd in the arena a distant sound
like flowing water. He stares at the mirror,
his mask face up on the table.
He's thinking how night after night,
one beer-soaked small-town gym
after another he wrestles for the crowd,
their tension focused on the mystery
of his face. And tonight, too tired to keep hiding,
he gives the word for his fall:
an eye gouge, drop-kick,
a figure-four-leg-lock into a body slam
and he lies pinned to the mat, mask stripped.
His opponent waves it like a severed head,
Mascaras rising at center ring,
rotating his face toward the silenced crowd
like a lighthouse beacon,
shining his burned, scarred skin.

For years I've searched his face for new lesions
the way I study soil for signs of spring.
Now his infection is so obvious
the neighborhood kids have stopped
riding their bicycles past his house,
Where else, he jokes, *but at the end of the road.*
I hand him prescriptions, referral names and numbers,
and he hands me the mask:
Don't worry about me, Richard,
wrestling is fixed,
the outcome of every fight
is known in advance.

IV.

What a Psychiatrist Remembers

Alzheimer's Unit

Every evening,
just when quiet comes,
she awakens on the prowl.
Men spared from longing
float like seaweed
and hear her chant,
relentless as the thousand
tongues of waves.
A few understand
her body's invitation,
the deep taste of salt.
But none recall
the night before,
reviving in her sea.
And when by chance
they kiss and click
like shells in the surf,
a door closes,
and their rhythm is an ocean
where memories swim with starlight
over the chanting swells.

First Break

In a time before tabloid news
when shooting pool was psychotherapy,
we drained long afternoons breaking the pack.
Dave wore a work shirt and overalls,
flashing a grin that tore his acned face
when he cocked his head and heard the voices taunt.
I was just a first year resident in a stiff dark suit,
too young to know
love can be sharp as the blade of a Bowie knife.

We played Eight Ball in the shattered light,
our young-man banter billed as treatment.
The voices started when his girl flew
out west, and I only half-believed he'd ever had her.
Between shots, in the slash of time,
he argued with the world he heard
and laughed the lonely laugh
of the only man who gets a joke.
At game's end, the black ball buried
in a corner, he'd stand heron-still,
only his fingers chalking the cue,
and I would rack the balls
and wait for him to break.

One afternoon she returned,
the blue-eyed, kilted girl next door,
the kind of beauty that spills blood.
We shot pool while her eyes studied him,
her voice cooing, *You're wonderful Dave,
but I'm not the one for you,*
while her hand snapped
the eight ball from cushion to cushion.

He chalked his stick and she vanished like blue dust.
Our game unfinished, we left the broken pack
on the perfect green table.

For months I tried to quiet the voices
with Thorazine, Stelazine, and Loxitane,
but their cuts were insoluble
and I sent him home, forgotten
until an ER call and a blood-soaked crotch,
his penis on a tray of ice.
All night, surgeons sewed skin
thin as angels' wings, and I restrained him
with leather and kept him
asleep with morphine.
When he woke a few days later
and I had to loosen his restraints,
the commands intensified
and he ripped the sutures in a single pull,
blood on both our hands,
nothing in my power with the strength to bind him.

Tools
—for Barry Stemlieb

They hang from the rack:
my father's spade saving last year's mud,
a long-tined rake, the swan-neck hoe.
Each spring, when earth warms and begs
me to open its dark skin, I carry them
past flowering apples and pears to the quiet
square of garden, to excite what lies buried
beneath the surface. The spade slices deep,
turns clay and compost in a wet, fertile dough
combed smooth by the rake's thin hand.
The graceful hoe chops dandelions
that intrude like obsessions
and waits patiently to scrape purslane
when it grows fast as jealousy in July.
I love their simple handles, the smooth taper
of oiled oak and ash, their honest grains
spiraling like a patient's thoughts.

    My psychiatrist tools are simple too:
a room with a closed door, a few chairs, pills,
and packets of words I cultivate like, *That hurts* or *Yes, I see*,
words that smooth a surface or dig up something dormant
like last year's seeds stirred from below
whispering green shoots before the first hope of warmth.

Woman with a Finger Stuck in her Nose

What was funny
wasn't where it was stuck,
or her phoning
Please, a surgeon,
my brain is leaking out!
No, the funny part was
the hospital operator
triaging her right
to Psychiatry.

It's comical, too
when you get your own
finger stuck somewhere
and your brain starts to ooze,
how someone lands
from out of the blue
with a cork,
some suture,
or a few words
that hold you together
like crazy glue,
solid as a kiss,
a joke,
a prayer.

Migration, 3 A.M.

My patient reels into Seven and a Half,
the room for the crazed and half-crazed.
Mid-twenties, vomit-flecked mouth,
bare feet, white boxer shorts,
her black spaghetti-strap T-shirt
has fallen below her breasts,
one tattooed with a monarch butterfly.

I find her a robe and cigarettes,
notice wrists bloodied from handcuffs,
a sutured slash up her forearm
fashioned for her husband:
He loves his truck more than me . . .
After three cigarettes
and an hour of drunken rambling
she screams, *Fuck off!*
All I can do is commit her.
So simple: my signature on pink paper.

Sleep/wake day/night disconnected,
ferocious hunger for a waffle piled with strawberries,
the doors whoosh open and rain smacks me.
I flip on the radio to the surprise of jazz,
wind in the trees like brushed drum beats.
I'm laughing, scat-singing her name,
imagining monarchs flying to Costa Rica.
And when I visit her in the morning
she will pause like a one-night lover
who doesn't remember my name.

Transference

I can't remember what he says
this first session, only his careful attention
and a sense he sees through my camouflage.
I feel I've known him a long time,
familiar as red in the maple outside
or the smell of leather on my father's skin.
When I cry, tissues are at hand,
and when I sob, he listens, alert,
silent, which comforts me and is sufficient.
And I feel closer to him than 50 minutes
should allow, a puzzled sensation
I've known him all my life.
Certain I have chosen wisely,
I reach out to say *Good bye Jerry*,
my dead father's name.

Crossing the Street
—from the painting by Giovanni Boldoni, 1842–1931

Crossing the street after rain,
empty hands in empty pockets,
I am a patient who arrives on time.
The office waits beyond white pines,
lower limbs broken off after living
too long without sun. I have watched
brown needles detach in fall,
wondered at patients stringing Christmas lights,
and tried to hope when spring
branches thrust green candles.

Crossing the street I am a glass
filled a fraction above the rim,
tension holding precarious before I spill.
I trample the corner feet have worn
brown in the grass, open the door
up the back stairway, clean
with the sweet smell of soap,
drag down a long, carpeted hall
to the late afternoon office.

Crossing my legs, I lean back,
eyes wandering — a photo of Erik Erikson,
shelves of hard bound books,
flowers arranged in a pewter vase,
and I remember the painting:
a woman crosses a cobblestone street
after the rain, black carriage,
black dog and dingy building behind her,

one cautious hand lifting
the hem of her black ruffled dress
revealing what she prefers to hide,
the other clutching an abundance of pink.
Yes, I cry, *yes*,
to be crossing the street
in a wet, gray world,
lips set to smile,
my arm like hers,
cradling a rose bouquet.

What a Psychiatrist Remembers

I remember rain hammering a green tin roof,
the light at each prescribed hour.

I remember perfumes and anxious sweat,
who preferred the big leather chair

and who liked to hide in the sofa's corner.
I remember watching hairlines recede,

weight gained and lost from faces
like snow drifted high and melted by sunlight.

I remember empty men who devoured my words
and those too full of themselves.

I remember invisible families
I could describe as if gazing at an old photo,

how people rehearsed new lines
like actors in a foreign city.

I remember women and men on fire
and the frozen who needed me for kindling.

I remember forgetting
a session with a man whose words

whipped me like his father's belt,
my small amnesias for anniversaries,

who said what when,
and how much my lapses hurt them.

I remember sitting like my patients
when time expired,

entire lives grasped in a 50-minute hour,
how at baffled moments

I leaned too far back in my rocker
and knew the fear of falling.

Rough Air

Patients straggle back
on schedule, rumpled and loose
as unpacked laundry, return
what they borrowed:
my small wooden clock,
the nautilus shell, a framed butterfly.
A few unfold soiled notes I signed
on crisp white paper weeks ago
with today's date and time.
They ask if I had a good trip,
thank me for coming back —
passengers praising the captain
when they stumble out
after two hours of turbulence.
If only I could take each one in my arms,
hold them long enough to say *Yes,*
I'm here, I thought of you at 30,000 feet,
remembered you at Van Gogh's portrait
of the sad Dr. Paul Gachet, tell them
the times I, too, was violated,
my life flying past at six miles a minute.

What Makes a Psychiatrist Cry

At ten past ten I hear the clock tick,
feel furnace air on my face,
watch a dust ball bounce the blonde wood floor.
I inspect my pen, wishing it could write
the story of why you're not here.
For six months you've scraped your knees
raw in the rough schoolyard of memory.
Now that you're gone without good bye,
I am alone with memories of loss:
last week's death of a dialysis patient,
the day I watched my father
float on the clear Caribbean
and knew for certain he was dying.
If you were here I'd hold these thoughts
like a wafer of glass between us,
light enough to balance without your notice,
and I would watch you rage and watch you cry,
my eyes wandering from your face to the clock,
fixing on the half-fallen storm window,
drifting outside to a white birch,
the yellowed leaves clinging tight
before their letting go.

Berlin Wall

I sit with my patient but can't tune in
to another painful story.
A July breeze sighs rugosa rose
and fresh cut grass through my open window.
Across the lawn, two tanned
and pony-tailed men lay brick
four stories up the new clinic wall,
so young, they still stroll
the thin scaffold without fear.
I drift back to the confused architecture
of early adolescence, when kids taunted
Berlin Wall! Berlin Wall!
across the wet summer my father began
his dying and my mother her 10-year grief.
It was the time I learned to daydream
out windows, cover loss with brick,
until I became a walled city,
the free world all around,
a barbed wire climb the only way out.

Dance Lesson

Spinning and tumbling,
hands held tight to a DSM,
racing through the routine
questions of sleep and sex,
twisting toward tobacco,
straining to split
grief from depression,
I perform compulsory moves,
even a moment, perhaps, of listening.
Finished in fifteen minutes,
speeding to jump
to diagnosis, I nail
my twisted landing
deep in corporate shadow.

                    But I remember
when psychiatry was ballet, how we danced
to Debussy and dressed technique
with beauty. Back then we studied
the moves of masters, waited for time
between beats, and danced slow
as the limping step of patient partners
whose gaze we held
just beyond reach of our hands.

Covert Operations

Sensing a first-born son,
    loved too much
to depend on them

for more than stories
    they can afford to tell,
patients view me

with night-vision glasses,
    a man who drags his feet
down foreign streets,

past Middle-Age
    churches, ruins lit by starlight
and a crescent moon

in pursuit of intelligence
    from the past.
And they've guessed

I ride trains facing backwards
    to see what is left behind:
crumbled chateaus and orchards,

the dark distillation of refineries
    stacked against gray rivers,
swans flying their secret, silvered tracks.

Jumpology

At every time when the subject agreed to jump, it was for me like a kind of victory.
　　　　　　　　—Philippe Halsman, photographer

And they are caught forever in mid-air:
Audrey Hepburn, legs splayed,
white blouse billowed,
arms clasped behind her back,
mouth in a smile of complete joy;
Marilyn Monroe in full body profile,
black fringed cocktail dress
clinging to her legs, hair flying,
mouth opened in a smile
men of the '50s could interpret
only one way;
even Richard Nixon an inch off the ground,
arms flapping like broken wings,
lips turned down, yet unmistakably a grin.

And how did Halsman provoke them to jump,
to fling their masks and go airborne
before the camera's expressionless eye?
I suspect he won them like a psychiatrist
with an array of empathic comments,
raising their attention with questions
a friend might fear to ask. And later,
when he hoped he held their trust,
heart pounding, fighting all inhibition,
the decisive moment
he asked them to leave the ground,
let go of words, the studied pose, and fly
toward the praise of light.

V.

What I Love

If You Ask Me My Name

I will say healer, priest,
turner of textbook pages,
searcher, listener, arrogant crow
costumed in white, reflecting moon.
My name is scared and foolish
and sometimes too tired to care.
I am death's reluctant lover,
a child's guide, mother, father,
hero and fool,
and if you like it simple,
doctor will do.

Sleight of Hand

Old as my grandmother,
she smiles up at me,
breath gentle and lulled,
her fears distracted
by my questions and patter.
I percuss her chest,
listen to her heart,
my style cool and entertaining
as any close-up magician
until I palpate her breast,
feel her flesh
like decayed leaves crushed
by time to a star of coal.
My fingertips define the borders,
sweat beads under my arms,
thoughts flash ahead
to the incision's red arc,
the yellow bottles of poison.
Her laughter breaks my trance:
You should have seen them when I was younger.
Oh for a stronger magic,
that I could wave my arms
and reach deep inside
my white coat pocket,
the mass vanished,
my hand a heaven of diamonds
over her generous breasts.

Obstetrics Ward, County Hospital

I slam the locker and dial Security.
Across the hall, fifty beds bulge
with the high tide of labor.
Grandmothers with boom boxes
boogie in the aisles
and sponge breasts of girls
who cry *mama, mama, mama.*
At any moment one will rise,
heave and stumble
past students and ultrasounds
to the corridor called Labor Line.
Babies burst out before their time
and midwives catch them above the slop
of blood and stool and amniotic fluid,
medical students thrilled by a footling breech,
a four-fingered hand, the drama of hemorrhage,
clamps, forceps and suture dancing
as child-mothers moan *mama, mama, mama.*
Cleaned and toweled, we give up
babies to grandmothers who live the struggles
of milk and blood on barren streets,
a cradle lined with bullets and broken glass.
And after legions of new lives have wailed
into this world, I wait for Security's safe delivery
to the parking lot, where the city heaves
its great contractions, and night labors hard
into morning.

Hospital Food

We lower a plastic tray on his ribs
as if food can stop the dying:
cold potato scooped like a snowball,
canned spinach oozing green,
microwaved chicken thigh.
I've watched anorectic men clog
N-G tubes with brown rice
and Kombacha mushroom tea,
listened to wives plead
Just make him take a few bites,
withstood lectures on macrobiotics
delivered by a Camel chain-smoker.
No, I've never seen hospital food
stop the dying.

Some days, worn and hungry,
I take refuge in smooth noodles
glistening black beans and red chilies,
fragrant sips of jasmine tea,
sweet white sesame balls the size of prayers.
And I think about the sick men
dissolving like tailpipes in the sea,
what they long to devour,
how we die without appetite
and the way we live with hungers
that consume our hearts like another kind of dying.

The Tailors of Children's Memorial
  —*after Beatrix Potter*

It is Christmas Eve
and our patient lies on the table
in twilight sleep. Gazing at a masked face
turned upside down, he hears a voice
that drifts like anesthesia, strokes him
gentle and steady as a grandfather clock:

In the time of swords and periwigs there lived a tailor in Gloucester. . .

The boy's thoughts drift to the tired old tailor
sewing the Mayor's Christmas coat
while Simpkin the cat captures mice
dressed in waistcoats of paduasoy and taffeta
and hides the last spool of cherry coloured twist.
His eyes close quiet as snow.

. . . The old tailor worked and worked until two days before Christmas, when he fell asleep before the fire, the coat unfinished, too sick to sew another stitch . . .

With the boy on his belly, our cheesecutter
shaves cloth from his buttocks,
OR light glowing through our fabric
like moonlight, gloved hands creating new flesh
to the beat of the anesthetist's voice.

. . . On Christmas Eve, the coat still in pieces, the mice came out from their homes in the wall and began to sew . . .

On blistered hands his father held to fire
two teams sew 5-0 chromic
with snips of scissors and snaps of clamps,

tiny needles hooking mouse-sized bites of skin,
fingers tying our finest knots, stitches so neat, so small,
they look as if little mice had made them.

...When the tailor woke on Christmas Day and unlocked his shop, there lay the most beautiful satin waistcoat anyone had ever seen. Beside a single unsewn buttonhole lay a note from the mice: "No more twist."

Our shop never runs short of suture
and we stitch for days without sleep,
hold flesh in our burning hands like silk,
possessed with the power to sew
the darkest seams.

. . . From then on, the luck of the Tailor of Gloucester changed. He grew quite stout and he grew quite rich and made the most wonderful waistcoats for the fine gentlemen of the country round.

We gather the instruments,
peel off gloves and plain green gowns,
untie masks and wonder
at new skin fashioned by hand.
And tomorrow, on Christmas Day,
we will wear our finest coats
against a threadbare world
even the tailors of Children's Memorial
lack the magic to mend.

Portrait of a Family Doctor

I observe the physician with the same diligence as he the disease.
                        —John Donne, *Devotions*

Piece-worker on the patient care line,
black bag empty as a new moon,
Marcus Welby not even a memory
as your back breaks like an old book.
Sweating six patients per hour,
exam rooms filled like flood plains,
bureaucrats in glass towers hoard your dollars
while subspecialists snigger
when you can't recall their narrow facts.
Eroded by paper work, there are moments
you reach deep into the current
that washed you here, hands clean
and cradling a new-born
or guiding the scope and snipping
a mushroom from the bowel's wet wall,
the deep pleasure of will
when a woman listens
and drowns her last cigarette.
And in early evening,
when coffee can't revive you,
you struggle to the surface and give
what you can: a few hurried words,
a hand on a shoulder,
a pill the color of your flesh.

Sleep Lab Meditation

They wander in like lost Buddhas,
awake when they wish to sleep.

Before their rest I bind them tight
to measure the strain of every breath,

anoint them with sensors
on scalp and chin.

Five rooms bear five seekers
who begin their journey never knowing

angels mistook Adam for immortal
before they saw him sleep.

Through the one-way mirror
I watch their eyes

grow calm as summer lakes,
surfaces shimmering in a breeze of dreams

blown by varieties of waking.
Reverie glows in green lines

on my monitors like threads
between underworld and paradise.

All night, patterns repeat
with the trance of prayers

until dawn startles the horizon
and I hum for shadows

to rejoin their bodies.
It is said that in heaven there is no sleep

and when I rouse my subjects
all swear they never slept.

Blighted Ovum

He might have introduced himself
before he slid his probe
deep into space I thought was heaven,
exploring like a robot for signs of life
on a barren planet.
They say life requires water,
but he ignored our tears,
preferring to study the monitor's
heartless white nebula
where our world spun light years away.

When he left my wife on her back,
his instrument still inside,
her bladder bursting like the first astronaut's,
the lab tech shuffled in
like a weightless woman returned to gravity.
Staring toward infinity, she pulled the probe
and granted permission to pee.
Sound doesn't carry in a vacuum,
though I thought I saw her lips say, *I'm sorry*,
her eyes tracking the lifeless space
frozen on a blackened screen.

Our Medical Marriage
—for Susanne

We kneeled on the bookstore floor
two students scanning the bodies
of new books, checking out
each other's *Principles*
of Internal Medicine.
Scores of textbooks later
we're a pair of pagers and missed dinners,
companions in sleep-deprived nights.
We suffered the long delay
before our only child while we ran
to slashed wrists and ODs,
sprinted from half-read journal
to school play to board meeting.
In conversation long as summer light
we talked patients and drugs,
recited the simple prayers of the dying,
learned how we both took medicine
as a life-long lover.

One hushed June evening in mid-life
scented rose and thick with fireflies,
the phone steals her.
I sit with my half-filled glass
and a life we knew we were choosing,
our marriage a joining of two strains
of mint, planted close, cross-pollinated
to form a single type, the small, unfailing
flowers arrayed in purple spikes
I can see most clearly
when I'm down on my knees.

After Watching *Chicago Hope*

Last night a beautiful widow,
face feathered with Van Gogh light,
stood by the ER window
as she mourned her father.
The surgeon listened omnipotent
and they fell in love.
Sometimes I yearn for drama,
wish someone would explode
my detached concern.
But most days, medicine is gardening
below a gray sky, the merciless light
shadowless, flat, weeds and rocks
exposed as I till row after row,
patients crumbling into earth,
the cold and sudden rain,
insistent threats of lightning,
and every so often, when my eyes
and back are bent to the ground,
sunlight falls on my neck,
soft and silent and unannounced.

What I Love
   —*after Stephen Dunn*

I love my long white coat, belted in the back,
deep pockets filled with tourniquet, tuning fork,
reflex hammer and pens; the pride of uniform
grown from short white to long blue and long gray,
until finally, long white and arrival as Chief,
each coat earned with tears and blood on my sleeves.
I love the purity of white,
as if the great whale's strength and mystery
and power surround my body,
the way each patient, even the most demented,
knows white coat means *doctor*.

I love the library's old book smell
and a new text's clean gloss,
the endless flow of journals, new data
that seem so solid before the ground moves
and grand theories yield to a few humble facts;
the miracle of MEDLINE, Silver Platter,
Grateful Med, everything known and unknown
for longer than I have searched or breathed,
the infinity of my ignorance.

I love the big words and their sounds:
Serratia, Pseudomonas, choreoathetosis,
how words shrink to CATS and SPECTS,
crits and Cipro and adenoCA,
the illusion: we control by naming.
And I would love the words even more
if I did not know their meanings,

the abbreviated way we dismiss people
as left hemis, diabetics, schizophrenics,
my shame for comfort I have stolen
beneath a word's cool shadow.

I love a stethoscope draped around my neck
casual as a towel at poolside,
my swoon for our tools: Queen's Square hammer,
ophthalmoscope, soundings my hands percuss,
weathermap shadows on ultrasound,
a cardiogram's sharp repetition,
the rolling sea in fathoms of brain waves.
Yet the tools I love most are my eyes
that measure in an instant, how sick, how well.

I love a nurse who knows the doses,
the patient and family's story,
moments in crisis we become each other's hands,
teamwork that appears sudden as a star.
I love the banter, the jokes, the sexual charge
so alive in the constant presence of death.
And because I am a hatmaker's son
I love a nurse's white winged cap.

I love to pretend I've saved a life
though I know it's just a postponement
before pronouncement and suffering's end
when I bend, humble and yielding.
I love the drama, keeping cool in crisis,
running a code, giving good advice,
the way each story shines a beam of humor
if I can place my mind at a certain angle,
the laughter that lets me go on.

I love my patients, not as a group, but one by one,
their varieties of trust below the surface,
permission to ask about blood and bowel movements,
lives and loves. And they come with their own yearning
questions I answer by listening without judgment,
the miracle that listening is sometimes enough.

I love to come home to my orchard when apples are ripe,
watch my daughter slice garlic
and my wife arrange lilies in a vase,
the vacation surprise that people can eat and pee,
walk without walkers or an IV pole.
And I love to take off my white coat, the stethoscope,
forget the big words and listening's weight,
all the sounds and smells and tests
of this life I have chosen,
and remember the white and bloodless world I knew
before I fell in love.

RICHARD M. BERLIN was born in 1950, grew up in Teaneck, New Jersey, and received his undergraduate and medical education at Northwestern University. His poetry appears monthly in "Poetry of the Times," a featured column in *Psychiatric Times*. An Associate Professor of Psychiatry at the University of Massachusetts Medical School, he has written extensively on the doctor-patient relationship, sleep disorders, and the psychiatric care of the medically ill. He lives with his wife and practices psychiatry in a small town in the Berkshire hills of western Massachusetts.